THE GIFTS
OF THE
Magi

Based On the Classic O. Henry Stories

THE GIFTS OF THE Magi

Based On the Classic O. Henry Stories

The Fireside Theatre

GARDEN CITY, NEW YORK

Copyright © 1984 Randy Courts and Mark St. Germain

Design by Maria Chiarino

Photos of Lamb's Theatre Company productions by Carol Rosegg.

ISBN 1-56865-117-1

Manufactured in the United States of America.

THE GIFTS OF THE MAGI was commissioned for development by the Lamb's Theatre Company, Carolyn Rossi Copeland, Executive Director. It received its premiere production at the Lamb's Theatre in New York City, on December 3, 1984. It was directed by Christopher Catt; the piano, vocal arrangements were by Steven M. Alper and Randy Courts; the incidental music was arranged by Steven M. Alper; the sets were by Michael C. Smith; the lighting was by Heather Carson; the costumes were by Hope Hanafin; the choreography was by Piper Pickrell; the production stage manager was Steve Zorthian; the assistant stage manager was Maude Brickner; the assistant to the executive director was Pamela Perrell; the technical director was Joseph Connell; the assistant to the technical director was Amy Darnton; and the casting was by McCorkle Casting, Ltd. The cast was as follows:

THE CITY: HIM . . . . Brick Hartney
THE CITY: HER . . . . .Lynne Winterstellar
WILLY . . . . .Michael Brian
JIM . . . . Jeff McCarthy
DELLA . . . . .Leslie Hicks
SOAPY . . . . .Bert Michaels

To Carolyn Rossi Copeland, who commissioned this musical and began a three-way collaboration that is its own gift.

Randy Courts
Mark St. Germain

Book and Lyrics by Mark St. Germain
Music and Lyrics by Randy Courts

THE GIFTS OF THE Magi

Based On the Classic O. Henry Stories

OPENING CAROL: STAR OF THE NIGHT

CITY HIM and CITY HER:

> STAR OF THE NIGHT
> WITH YOUR BRIGHT HOLY LIGHT
> LEAD ME ON MY WAY
> THROUGH DESERT SANDS
> THROUGH THE SNOW-COVERED LANDS
> TO BETHLEHEM
> OII SIIINING STAR, SHINING STAR
>
> ALL GOOD THINGS
> OF WISDOM AND KINGS
> WE BRING WITH JOY
> WHILE THE HEAVENS SIGH
> AND A CHOIR ON IIIGII SINGS GLORIA
> GLORIA, GLORIA
>
> TO A LITTLE BOY
> IN A LITTLE TOWN
> WHOSE NAME MEANS SAVIOR
> WE BRING THIS CROWN
> GLORIA, GLORIA, GLORIA

(*Audience enters to see and hear the caroling of City Him and Her as they sing STAR OF THE NIGHT, and other carols if desired. City Him and Her sing from a bare stage divided by a simple curtain, and sing a capella. As lights gradually dim, focusing more and more on them, the cries of a newsboy, Willy Porter, are heard in the distance, louder as the song reaches conclusion. Willy moves through the audience to the stage, producing a newspaper from his bag with a conjurer's skill*)

WILLY (*calling out to audience*): Extra! Extra! (*Quoting headlines*) "Brooklyn Trolley Runs Wild," "Teddy R. Calls Football Hooliganism," "Riots in St. Petersburg," "Forty Thousand Bills Paid For Aristocrat Carnation" (*Willy arrives on stage, tipping his hat to City Him and Her, who nod their acquaintance and move off the stage, leaving it to Willy. A piano accompaniment has risen, assuming a melody of its own. Willy crosses to his newspaper sales area, indicated by a stack of newspapers and a few meager belongings*)—All for a penny, folks. And here's the real news: Only two more days to Christmas!

SONG: GIFTS OF THE MAGI

WILLY:

> STORIES OF THE DAY
> SINGING OUT THE LEAD
> NOTHING MUCH TO SAY
> JUST A LOT TO READ
>   Papers! Papers Here!
> WINTER TAKES MY SONG
> THROUGH THE MORNING AIR
> CARRIES IT ALONG
> EVERYWHERE
>
> WHAT WOULD YOU PREFER
> INK UPON A PAGE
> OR THAT I COULD   (*Stage lights go on*)
>   STIR
> CHRISTMAS ON A   (*City Him and Her move*
>   STAGE   *to either side of*
>   *curtain*)
> SHOULD I TELL MY   (*Motions Jim onstage from*
>   TALE   *left*)
> WILL YOU PLAY A
>   PART

KNOWING IT'S FOR   *(Motions Della onstage*
   SALE   *from right)*
BUY IT WITH YOUR
   HEART

AND THOUGH I WILL
   NOT
   SWEAR A VOW
THAT ALL I TELL IS   *(Jim and Della move into*
   TRUE   *a loving embrace)*
I SWEAR THAT IT ALL
   COULD
   HAPPEN NOW
   TO YOU

(Willy turns, crosses to Jim and Della, and a pin spot illuminates the direction of his gaze as he stares at them. To audience) You might not think it from looking at 'em but those two folks holding onto each other are married. *(Jim and Della separate, freeze)* And you might not guess it from looking at 'em, but the holding on is getting harder and harder. Introducing the Dillinghams, Jim and Della. *(Through next verse of song, Willy crosses between Jim and Della)*

I CAN STOP A CLOCK   *(Makes watch appear in*
                         his hand, puts it
MAKE THE SUN   *in Jim's pocket)*
   APPEAR
FILL A CITY BLOCK   *(Pulls gently on Della's*
FREEZE A SINGLE   *hair, which is*
   TEAR   *put up on her head. It*
                         tumbles about
                         her shoulders)

(*Willy snaps his fingers, unfreezes Jim and Della. Jim puts his coat on, Della helping him*)

DELLA: I'll come with you.

JIM: I'm only going for the paper; I'll be right back.

DELLA: Maybe you'll need help. Maybe the want ads will be so thick it will take the two of us to carry them—

JIM: Maybe you should go back to bed till you stop dreaming.

DELLA (*kisses him*): Not unless I have company. (*Pause*) You didn't sleep again last night, did you?

JIM: I did, a little. But I'm fine.

DELLA: Hurry home. I'll keep my fingers, toes and eyes crossed for you. Good luck—

JIM (*stops, turns to her*): I don't need luck. And I don't need crossed fingers. I don't need anything but a job. (*Turns to walk away, looks embarrassed*) Do you have any money for the paper? (*Della gives Jim a penny; Jim impulsively embraces her. They freeze*)

WILLY (*singing to audience*):
LOOK AND YOU WILL SEE
HOPE IS ALL AGLOW
DREAMS OF WHAT CAN BE
SETTLE LIKE THE SNOW
YOU'RE ABOUT TO KNOW
OF THE GIFTS OF THE MAGI

(*All begin moving onstage; Jim approaches Willy for a paper; Della begins to comb her hair*)

WILLY (*tips cap to audience*): Willy Porter; pleased to meetcha.

JIM: Good morning Willy. (*Takes out a penny*) How thick are your classifieds today?

WILLY: Save your brown, Mr. D. (*Indicates curtain upstage which City Him and Her pull back to reveal a newspaper covered park bench*) Read the park bench.

JIM: Much obliged. (*Claps him on the shoulder; moves to the bench where Soapy Smith, unseen, is stretched out and hidden with newspapers. City Him and Her cross, passing Jim, approaching Willy*)

HER: Good morning, William.

HIM: Morning, Willy. (*Indicates Jim*) Still looking for work, is he?

WILLY: You know better than I do. Will he find it?

HIM: He might.

HER: Then again, he might not.

(*Willy crosses between them*)

WILLY (*to audience*): Nearly four million strangers in this little island off the Jersey Coast. We don't have the time to introduce you to all of them, even if you had the memory for it. So let's make things easy for everybody: Meet the City Him and Her.

HIM (*presentationally*): New . . .

HER (*undercuts*): York. The Public.

HIM (*cuts in, bows*): Utilities.

WILLY: Pared to a pair.

HIM: From the tip of the Tenderloin—

HER: To the barrens beyond 145th Street—

HIM: The height of Times Tower—

HER: To the cavities of the underground drilled with train tracks—

HIM: The march of the markets—

HER: The crawl of culture—

HIM: And metropolitan vice we can be proud of!

WILLY: Everywhere; ever present, wall upon wall of indifference.

HIM AND HER (*grudging*): That too.

WILLY: The City.

HIM (*moves to audience*): We've met, haven't we? I never forget a face.

HER (*to audience*): Unfortunately, it's a solitary talent. (*City Him and City Her move, clearing sight lines of park bench and Jim*)

WILLY: —Now just one more—(*Jim has picked up a paper from the bench. Soapy Smith, now revealed, sits upright, wiping his eyes of sleep*)

JIM: I'm sorry—I didn't see you.

WILLY (*to audience*): Say hello to Soapy Smith.

SOAPY (*yawning; addresses Jim*): Don't think twice about it. Time to get up anyways. (*Looks at paper in Jim's hand, and its date*) It's December, isn't it? (*Jim makes a gesture to give Soapy the paper; Soapy waves it back to Jim and, instead, takes the penny Jim holds still in his hand. All onstage freeze, except Willy*)

WILLY:
> AND THOUGH I SPEAK A PARABLE
> OF PEOPLE WHO WOULD FLY
> WOULD IT BE SO TERRIBLE TO TRY
> COME AND TRY, OH
>
> WHAT COULD MAKE A KING
> TRAIL A STAR ABOVE
> GIVE UP EVERYTHING
> MAYBE IT WAS LOVE
> LOVE IS WHAT WE BRING

ALL:
> AND THOUGH WE WILL NOT SWEAR A VOW
>   THAT ALL WE TELL IS TRUE
> WE SWEAR IT ALL COULD HAPPEN NOW
> TO YOU

WILLY:
> ARE WE FACT ARE WE MYTH
> WE WILL ANSWER YOU WITH
> JUST ONE

ALL:

> LOOK AND YOU WILL SEE
> HOPE IS ALL AGLOW
> DREAMS OF WHAT CAN BE
> SETTLE LIKE THE SNOW
> COULD YOU EVER GIVE
> EVERYTHING YOU OWN
> EVERYTHING YOU TOUCH
> ALL YOU'VE EVER LOVED
> ALL YOU'VE EVER KNOWN
> WOULD IT BE AS MUCH
> AS THE GIFTS OF THE MAGI

WILLY:

> WILL IT BE AS MUCH
> AS THE GIFTS OF THE MAGI

(*At song's conclusion, Della exits; Willy crosses to his newspaper area. Jim exits through audience*) Papers here; "Tunnel Diggers Threaten Strike," "Bernhardt Bids New York Adieu" . . . Mr. D. —(*Jim, moving past him, stops*)

JIM: Willy?

WILLY: I've got a good feeling in my bones today. (*Jim smiles, exits. City Her, followed by City Him, move closer to Willy*)

HER (*sarcastic*): You're not dressed warmly enough.

HIM (*to Willy*): Will you be needing us?

WILLY: Not just yet.

HIM (*puts out an arm for her*): To Pulitzer Fountain at the Plaza; let's be a crowd and feed the pigeons.

HER (*takes his arm, but pulls him in another direction*): To Hell's Gate, 86th Street. Let's be a riot. (*City Her and Him exit*)

SOAPY (*crosses to Willy*): Thank you for the bedding, Willy my boy. (*Folding up some of the newspapers that covered him*)

WILLY: Thank me with the penny you cadged from Jim Dillingham. That guy's flat broke as you are, Soapy, but even worse—he *wants* to work.

SOAPY (*shudders*): Some people go to such extremes. (*To penny, which he takes out of his pocket*) See you again, sometime. (*Hands it to Willy*)

WILLY (*conspiratorially*): Just saw a couple of swells heading East on Eighth—

SOAPY (*tips hat to Willy*): I appreciate the illumination, Willy my boy, and I'm off. (*Soapy does a vibrant little tap step, at the same time removing his hat. His face changes from a pleased expression to a woeful one. With hat held in front of him, begging, he walks offstage with an exaggerated limp. As Willy says the following, he sets up the Dillingham flat: two chairs and a table with breakfast coffee cups on it*)

WILLY (*to audience*): You hear that sound? Listen again. It's the sound of a page being turned and a breath being held in the furnished flat of the Dillinghams. Round this time of morning, it's all you will hear. Until—(*Jim and Della have entered and sit across the table from each other. Jim scanning the paper's want ads and Della watching anxiously*)

JIM: There's one possibility. (*Folds paper, puts it down*)

DELLA: Good!

JIM: Better than nothing, I suppose.

DELLA: Of course it is! Jim, this could be just what you're looking for.

JIM: Della—

DELLA: I can just see it. (*Della rises through this and crosses behind Jim*) You'll start out as a clerk, or a clerk to a clerk, and before you know it, the boss clerk notices your work and recommends you to the manager, and the manager mentions you to the president, and the president says: "Keep an eye on that Dillingham," until one day the vice president gets run over by a horse when he's reaching for a penny in the gutter—

JIM: Della!

DELLA: So the president says, "Let's give that Dillingham a go"— and you're wildly successful, of course—(*Della moves back to her chair*)

JIM: Of course.

DELLA: And one night we're at the opera, the four of us. (*Jim shoots Della a questioning look*) The president's married—and suddenly he clutches at his heart, falling to the floor at the exact moment Carmen is stabbed—

JIM: Good Lord!

DELLA: —You lean over him, loosening his stiff collar, trying to shake some life into his old and wrinkled body, and all he can

say, loud enough for the whole balcony to hear, is "Dillingham—
The company is yours." (*Della mimes closing her eyes, dying with
a short gasp*)

JIM (*pause*): Would you please not do this so early in the morning?

DELLA: There's always a chance—

JIM: Della! I HAVEN'T EVEN GOTTEN AN INTERVIEW YET!
(*Pause*) And you know I don't like opera. (*They laugh. Jim rises,
putting folded paper under his arm. He puts on his coat*): I want
to get down there before they open.

DELLA (*putting arms around his neck*): Can't you stay a little while?

JIM: It's late—

DELLA: It's early.

JIM (*kisses her*): I'll be back as soon as I can.

DELLA (*teasing*): As soon as you get that job!

JIM: Don't say that; I may never come back.

DELLA: Dress warmly; it must be freezing out there. Do you have
your gloves?

JIM: Right here.

DELLA: Oh, Jim—you should see the gloves Mr. Murphy on the first
floor gave to Mrs. Murphy. Fur-lined, sable she says. She's so
proud of them she's wearing them in the hallways now. I don't
know how they could have afforded such a pair—

JIM: I'm going. I don't have time to be sitting around here all day.

DELLA: I know you don't. Jim, will you be home later for some lunch?

JIM: I doubt it.

DELLA: Then let me make you something—

JIM: Would you stop? I have more to worry about than lunch, don't I? How should I know when I'll be home. You think I'm going to stop looking for work just to get back here so you have company?

DELLA: Jim—

JIM: What now?

DELLA (*pause*): I wasn't hinting for gloves. (*Pause*) I don't want them. Really.

JIM: Goodbye. (*Jim exits the apartment, enters the street*)

WILLY: Good luck, Mr. D. (*Willy freezes the action*)

SONG: JIM AND DELLA

WILLY:

> THERE ONCE WERE TWO SCHOOLKIDS
> OUT IN THE WHEAT BELT
> HELD HANDS AT RECESS AND WALKED
>   HOME REAL SLOW

DELLA:

> SECOND GRADE

JIM:

NO ONE AS PRETTY AS SHE
IN THE WHOLE WORLD

WILLY:

OR IN THEIR TOWN OF TWO HUNDRED OR
SO
AND THEY SWORE FROM THE

JIM:

SIXTH GRADE

DELLA:

VALENTINE'S DAY

JIM:

NEAR THE SWING IN THE BACKYARD

WILLY:

THEY'D MARRY

DELLA:

FOREVER

WILLY:

BE HAPPY
AND WEALTHY AND WISE

JIM:

WE'D BUY THINGS FOR OUR FOLKS

DELLA:

HAVE A HOUSE FULL OF KIDS

JIM and DELLA:

IN A CITY SO BIG AND SO FULL OF
SURPRISE

WILLY:

AND WHEN FAMILY AND FRIENDS WOULD
JUST
CHUCKLE AND SAY

DELLA:

THERE'S NO WAY

JIM:

WAIT AND SEE WHEN YOU GROW

WILLY:

JIM AND DELLA SAID NOTHING,
THEY'D SMILE AND THEY'D KNOW
THEY WERE RIGHT

JIM:

WE WERE DIFFERENT

DELLA:

AND SPECIAL

WILLY:

AND YOUNG
WITH A LOVE THAT THEY KNEW
WOULD BE MORE THAN ENOUGH
IN A WORLD THAT WAS RIGHT
AS THEY KNEW THEY WERE RIGHT
AND IN LOVE

WILLY:

CAME GRADUATION

JIM:

CAME THE PROPOSAL

WILLY:

SHE CAME DOWN THE AISLE

DELLA:

AND I WALKED IT REAL SLOW

JIM:

SEVENTEEN

DELLA:

NO ONE AS HANDSOME AS JIM IN THE
    WHOLE WORLD

WILLY:

NO ONE SO FRIGHTENED

JIM:

MY KNEES RATTLED SO

WILLY:

THEIR FIRST TRIP ON THE

JIM:

RAILROAD

DELLA:

MOM AND PAPA

WILLY:

SAID THEY'D WRITE, AND THEY DID

DELLA:

FOR AWHILE

JIM:

PLEASE SEND MONEY

DELLA:

GOOD PROSPECTS

WILLY:

AND OTHER SUCH LIES

JIM:

YES THE CITY WAS BIG

DELLA:

BUT NO ROOM FOR KIDS

JIM and DELLA:

EACH DAY WAS SO LONG AND SO FULL OF
   SURPRISE

WILLY:

AND THEY BOTH WERE SURPRISED TO START
   QUARRELING AT NIGHT

JIM and DELLA:

LET'S NOT FIGHT

JIM:

CAN'T YOU WATCH WHAT YOU SAY

WILLY:

JIM AND DELLA SAID LITTLE, AND THOUGHT
   OF THE DAYS

   WHEN THEY WERE RIGHT
   THEY WERE DIFFERENT

DELLA:

   AND SPECIAL

JIM:

   AND YOUNG

WILLY:

   WITH A LOVE THAT THEY HOPED
   WOULD BE MORE THAN ENOUGH
   IN A WORLD THAT WAS LESS
   EVERYDAY THERE WAS LESS
   OF THEIR LOVE

(*Jim and Della return to their frozen positions and Willy breaks the freeze*)

JIM: Thank you, Willy.

(*Jim and Della exit. City Him and Her enter and watch Jim exit*)

HIM: My my my. The young man seems a bit down at the mouth, doesn't he?

WILLY: A holiday can be a painful thing when you have no work to take a holiday from.

HER: It doesn't seem at all like the holidays to me.

WILLY: Why is that?

HER: No snow; or haven't you noticed? Can't tell Christmas from the Fourth of July without snow.

WILLY: I wouldn't say that. Haven't you noticed anything peculiar on the streets lately?

HER: More peculiar than usual?

HIM: Come to think of it, I have noticed a great deal of suspiciously civilized behavior.

WILLY: That's the tip-off to Christmas, all right. It's a seasonal virus, you could say.

HER: I haven't caught it.

WILLY: Maybe; maybe not. This bug shows itself in some mighty odd ways.

SONG: CHRISTMAS TO BLAME

WILLY:

I JUST SAW A COP IN BLUE
TEAR A TICKET UP IN TWO
BUT THERE WAS NO BRIBE OR DAME
SO IT MUST BE CHRISTMAS THAT'S TO
BLAME

ALL:

JINGLE BELLS, JINGLE BELLS
JINGLE ALL THE WAY

HIM:

INMATES DOWN AT CITY HALL
SPEAKING HONESTLY TO ALL
PEOPLE WONDER WHAT'S THEIR GAME
BUT IT MIGHT BE CHRISTMAS THAT'S TO
BLAME

ALL:

THERE IS SOMETHING IN THE HOLLY
ACTIVATES THE FOLLY INSIDE YOUR BRAIN
SOMETHING FORCES YOU TO SMILE
AND SLOWLY BUBBLES OUT THE BILE LIKE
   PINK CHAMPAGNE
OH COME ALL YE FAITHFUL

WILLY:

BARKEEPS DON'T SERVE WATERED ALE

HIM:

BUTCHERS EVEN UP THEIR SCALE

HER:

LANDLORDS GET A TOUCH OF SHAME

ALL:

SO IT MUST BE CHRISTMAS THAT'S TO
   BLAME

DON'T BLAME US
BLAME THE DAY
MISANTHROPES SEE MISTLETOE AND MELT
   AWAY

DECK THE HALLS WITH BOUGHS OF HOLLY

DON'T YOU FEAR IF YOU FEEL GOOD
DON'T BELEAGUER BROTHERHOOD
IT WILL QUICKLY DISAPPEAR
ALL IT MEANS IS CHRISTMAS
YES IT MEANS THAT CHRISTMAS TIME IS
   HERE

AND IT GOES BEFORE YOU KNOW IT
ALL THE HO-HO-HO-ING AND FA LA LA

HIM:

DON'T YOU THINK IT IS A PITY

HER:

THIS IS NEW YORK CITY NOT SHANGRI-LA

ALL:

GOOD KING WENCESLAS LOOKED OUT
ON THE FEAST OF STEPHEN

DON'T YOU FEAR IF YOU FEEL GOOD
DON'T BELEAGUER BROTHERHOOD
IT WILL QUICKLY DISAPPEAR
ALL IT MEANS IS

HER:

YES IT MEANS THAT

HIM:

IT JUST MEANS THAT

WILLY:

ALL IT MEANS IS

ALL:

YES IT MEANS THAT CHRISTMAS TIME IS

HER

(*distastefully*): JINGLE BELLS, JINGLE BELLS

HIM

(*enthusiastically*): DECK THE HALLS WITH
BOUGHS OF HOLLY

WILLY:

GOOD KING I FORGOT HIS NAME

ALL:

YES IT MEANS THAT CHRISTMAS TIME IS
HERE

(*Collective sigh. At conclusion of CHRISTMAS TO BLAME, lights change*)

WILLY: Broadway and 20th. Mid-morning on a busy street corner. (*Willy turns to look at Him and Her, who have been dawdling after the song's conclusion*) I said "busy." (*City Him and Her, affronted, exit. Soapy Smith enters*) Enter Soapy Smith . . .

SOAPY (*woeful, hat in hand, looks about until he spots City Him reentering in the guise of an affluent gentleman*): Excuse me, Sir. But could you spare a medicinal coin for my poor great grandmother's cough syrup?

HIM: I'm terribly sorry. (*Exits*)

SOAPY (*calling out after him*): She chokes on sympathy: the old dame needs cash!

WILLY (*at proscenium*): The City goes about its business; strolling, skipping, swaggering, scurrying, sneaking by—each man convinced the town is his and his alone. (*City Her enters in the guise of a society woman*)

SOAPY (*stopping her*): Pardon me, good lady—but could you spare a samaritan's silver for my poor blind great grandmother's hypercritical anatomical operation?

HER (*passing him by; exiting*): I believe not.

SOAPY: If you don't believe that one I have plenty more. (*City Him enters dressed as a stooped, old man. When he speaks, it is with an Irish lilt, and it is quite clear he is senile. Soapy stops him*)

One moment, kind sir, but could you spare a final coin for my poor, blind, dead great grandmother's funeral accommodations?

HIM: A coin?

SOAPY: A coin.

HIM: Save a penny every day, plant it in your ear, wash your hands and don't ever tickle strange fish. (*Soapy stares at him, reaches into his own pocket, turning it inside out, and gives him his last penny, motioning him to move off*)

SOAPY (*watching him go*): This city pulls 'em in like a magnet. (*Notices Willy has been observing*) The time has come again, William: I am running out of relatives. (*Sits on stage edge*)

WILLY (*crossing to him*): What time is that, Soapy?

SOAPY: The time for my annual holiday.

WILLY: You're going to get yourself locked up in jail again, I take it?

SOAPY: Jail to you; vacation to me. Three months on the Island. Three months of assured bed, board and company.

WILLY: What's wrong with a charity flophouse?

SOAPY: Every bed of charity has its bath, my friend. Every bowl of soup and slice of bread its private and personal inquisition. I prefer to be a guest of the law, which, though it is conducted by its own peculiar rules, doesn't much meddle in your personal affairs. (*In speaking, Soapy has taken off his hat, shaking it off. Her enters dressed as an old woman. She smiles sweetly, drops a coin into Soapy's overturned hat*)

HER: Merry Christmas to you. (*Exits*)

SOAPY: Good heavens! (*Takes coin out of his hat as if it's red hot, hands it to Willy*) Take this at once!

WILLY: But why?

SOAPY: A man can't be arrested for vagrancy with funds in his pocket! (*Exits through audience*)

WILLY: Papers here! (*Shouting headlines*) "First Neon Lights In Times Square"—(*Lights change; Willy directly addresses audience*) Special edition. (*Speaks headline*) "Girl in Love, Frantic." "Man Out of Work, Desperate." (*Lights rise on Della, standing frozen before City Him as butcher delivering meat*) Read all about it.

DELLA: Seventeen cents for two chops, Mr. Vincent? What's the price of meat coming to?

HIM: But free delivery, Mrs. Dillingham, not included in your price.

DELLA (*handing package back*): That's so kind of you, but would you take a few pennies off if you took them back to the store and I delivered them to me myself? (*Him looks at Della balefully. Lights up on Jim, as he enters an office looking for work. Him and Della freeze*)

WILLY: —Turn to page two . . . (*Her enters; she is a secretary, ungainly, officious and extremely taken by Jim*)

HER: Mr. . . .

JIM: Dillingham. James Dillingham.

HER: Mr. Hargrove will see you soon, Mr. Dillingham.

JIM: I appreciate it. (*Takes out his watch, looks at it, returns it to pocket*)

HER: Such a handsome face . . . on that watch.

JIM: Isn't it? From my great-grandfather to my grandfather to my father to me. It's our family fortune.

HER: It's very, excuse the expression, virile, Mr. Dillingham.

JIM: Thank you.

HER: Tell me. Is that "Mr." as in "Mr. and Mrs." or "Mr." as in "Lonely?" (*Her gives Jim a toothy smile; they freeze as Della and Him on other side of stage come to life. The pattern continues throughout the scene. In order to enhance the flow, the scenes are played simply, without excess movement*)

HIM: We're not talking baloney here, Mrs. Dillingham; the price of meat's gone up . . .

DELLA: But so much!

HIM: You got a problem with the cut of my chops, you come to me. You got a problem with the price, talk to the cows.

DELLA: I don't think the cows would miss a penny or two, do you, Mr. Vincent?

HIM (*sighs*): Mrs. Dillingham; why am I the one always on the hook? (*They freeze*)

JIM: I'm married.

HER: Oh?

JIM: To the most beautiful girl in New York City.

HER: How . . . nice. (*They freeze*)

HIM: How can I say "no" to such a pretty woman, Mrs. Dillingham? For you, sixteen cents.

DELLA: Thank you, Mr. Vincent. (*They freeze*)

JIM: And you, ma'am? Are you married?

HER: Don't get personal with me, Mister! (*They freeze*)

HIM: I have some nice fat turkeys . . .

HER: Daddy will see you *when* he can.

DELLA: I don't think so.

HIM: Merry Christmas, then. (*Exits*)

HER: Take a seat.

DELLA: Thank you!

JIM: Thank you; I'll wait. (*Jim sits. Della reaches into her apron, scooping out pennies that she's stored there, sits to count them*)

DELLA: I can't wait! Let's see—twenty-five cents plus the one, plus
five, that's thirty-one. Is that a penny or a dime? Oh, a penny.
Thirty . . . (*She has lost her place. Pause*) One, two, three . . .

SONG: *HOW MUCH TO BUY MY DREAM*

JIM:
I WAIT EACH DAY IN AN ENDLESS LINE
ON A CHAIR WHOSE BACK IS BROKEN DOWN
    WITH WEAR
I CROSS MY LEGS AS IF ALL IS FINE
AND I MASK MY FACE TO COVER ANY CARE
I GIVE MY WATCH A MOST CASUAL GLANCE
I PRETEND THAT I STILL HAVE ONE MORE
    CHANCE
BUT I KNOW THAT I DON'T, SO ALL DAY LONG
I PRETEND THAT I STILL FEEL CONFIDENT
    AND STRONG

I WAS THINKING ONCE UPON ANOTHER DAY
BACK WHEN MY DAYS WERE LAZY
I WAS THINKING I WOULD ALWAYS HAVE MY
    WAY
BUT I WAS THINKING CRAZY

USED TO BE THE FELLOW READY WITH A
    JOKE
SMALL POND, BIG FISH
NOW I'M ONLY ONE OF SEVERAL MILLION
    FOLK
LEFT WITH A FADING WISH

HOW DO YOU HOLD ONTO SMOKE
WHERE IS THE EDGE OF THE EARTH

WHY WOULD YOU LAUGH WHEN YOUR LIFE
  IS THE JOKE
AND WHAT WOULD A DREAM BE WORTH

HOW MUCH TO BUY MY DREAM
A NICKEL OR A TOKEN
WHAT PRICE WOULD DEPEND IT WOULD
  SEEM
ON WHETHER THE DREAM IS BROKEN

DELLA (*counting*): A dollar, a dollar ten, a dollar twenty, twenty five
—Isn't there any more silver here? A dollar . . . (*Has lost
place*) One, two, three . . .

JIM:

EVER NOTICE PEOPLE ON A CROWDED
  STREET
QUICKLY WALKING BY YOU
SEEMS THEY NEVER NOTICE ANYTHING BUT
  FEET
BUT BROTHER I TELL YOU I DO

I SEE THE TROUBLE IN A SMILE AND JUST
  BEHIND THE EYES
I SEE MYSELF
REACHING FOR AN ANSWER TO A DREAM
  THAT LIES
UP ON THE HIGHEST SHELF

HOW DO YOU KNOW WHO YOU ARE
WHERE IS YOUR PLACE ON THE EARTH
WHY WOULD YOU FOLLOW A VANISHING
  STAR
AND WHAT WOULD A DREAM BE WORTH

HOW MUCH TO BUY MY DREAM
A MIRACLE UNSPOKEN
WHAT PRICE WOULD DEPEND IT WOULD
   SEEM
ON WHETHER THE DREAM IS BROKEN

LIKE A NEW FROST UPON THE CITY
COVERS UP THE GRIME
LONG LOST, MORE'S THE PITY
ALL MY DREAMS ARE COVERED UP WITH TIME

DELLA: A dollar ninety-seven, is that all? It weighed so much; there has to be more than that . . .

HER (*enters behind Jim*): Mr. Hargrove won't be able to see you.

JIM: But I've been waiting all day! (*Knock on the door from Della's side of stage*)

HIM (*outside; voice only*): Landlord, Mrs. Dillingham.

JIM: Can I come back? Let me talk to him, at least—

HIM: I'm collecting early 'cause of the holiday. You have the rent?

DELLA (*disguising her voice*): Mrs. Dillingham's not here.

HIM (*sighs*): When will she be back?

DELLA: December twenty-sixth.

HER: He isn't here. Mr. Hargrave left early to buy a Christmas present for his wife. Good day. (*Exits*)

DELLA (*looking at her change*): A dollar ninety-seven!

(*Jim crosses back into the center*)

JIM:

MAYBE I SHOULD RUN AWAY AND NOT COME
   BACK
FIND SOME PRIDE TO BORROW
CALL IT A DAY. GO HOME AND HIT THE SACK
SLEEP THROUGH MY TOMORROW

IT'S AMAZING HOW A NIGHT OF REST CAN
   CHANGE THE PACE
WHEELS START TURNING
A MAN IS GOOD FOR NOTHING MORE THAN
   WASTING SPACE
WHENEVER HIS DREAM STOPS BURNING

HOW DO YOU HOLD ONTO SMOKE
WHERE IS THE EDGE OF THE EARTH
WHY WOULD YOU LAUGH WHEN YOUR LIFE
   IS THE JOKE
AND WHAT WOULD A DREAM BE WORTH

HOW MUCH TO BUY MY DREAM
A NICKEL OR A TOKEN
WHAT PRICE WOULD DEPEND IT WOULD
   SEEM
ON WHETHER THE DREAM IS BROKEN

SOMETIMES WHEN YOU SLEEP A DREAM
   GOES BY
BUT A MAN'S GOTTA BE WIDE AWAKE TO SEE
   ONE DIE

DELLA: There just has to be more. (*Lights out on Jim and Della. Lights up on Soapy: looking at imaginary restaurant*)

WILLY (*to audience*): "Gastronomere's Continental Cuisine," where gathered nightly are the choicest products of the grape, the silkworm and the protoplasm—(*Him, dressed as a policeman, enters, is stopped by Soapy*)

SOAPY: Tell me, Officer; how hard would the hairy arm of the law come down on a gent with empty pockets who filled his belly full (*gestures to restaurant*) at such a chophouse?

HIM (*eyeing Soapy*): I'd say the gentleman in question would be looking at six to eight weeks on the Island.

SOAPY: Six to eight, you say? (*Calculates*) Would a double dessert stiffen the sentence?

HIM: To three months, all told, it well might.

SOAPY: Sold! Thank you, your honor.

HIM: You'd better watch yourself, bub. (*Exits through audience*)

SOAPY: Watch me yourself, my friend. May your beat tonight be circular, for I hope to make your acquaintanceship again. (*City Her, dressed as Hostess, comes out through imaginary restaurant front door, lugging a garbage can*) A pleasant good evening to you . . . and your lovely can.

HER: Scraps are given out at the kitchen door. (*She leaves can and exits*)

WILLY (*from his area, having observed it all*): This joint a little too cosmopolitan for you, Soapy?

SOAPY: Cosmopolitan? So's a piece of flypaper. No, my problem was that I came on too nice to them. You can't afford to be polite if you want to enter polite society.

WILLY: You don't say.

SOAPY: I do say. Show any manners and you're a marked man. The upper class can't stay upper unless most folks are underneath 'em. (*Soapy sits on garbage can, straightening his outfit*)

SONG: THE RESTAURANT

SOAPY:

> IF YOU WANT TO DINE WHERE FOOD IS FINE
> AND FOLKS ARE EVEN FINER
> WHERE YA DON'T NEED KNIVES TO CUT
> YOU JUST NEED CHAT
> WHERE THE CLOTHES ARE ALL DESIGNER
> AND THE SHOES ALL HAVE A SHINER
> KEEP YOUR NOSE HELD UP AS HIGH AS
> KITES A FLYIN' IN THE SKY
> KEEP YOUR NOSE HELD UP AS HIGH
> AS YOUR HIGH HAT

(*City Him and Her enter, he as Garcon, she as Hostess. They set table and chair. From his pocket, Him removes silverware, wipes it carefully, sets the table as Her pulls napkin and bud vase from her clothing*)

HIM and HER:

> OUR CHORE IS TO SERVE AND POUR
> OUR JOB IS TO CATER
> SEE US IN A FRENZYFUL FUSS

WHEN A FELLOW TURNS TO BELLOW FOR HIS

SOAPY:

WAITER!

(*Soapy pops his hat; turns to enter restaurant, is met by Her*)

SOAPY: Table singular, and shake your bustle.

HER: Excuse me, Sir. (*Points to Soapy's shoes, which have gaping holes in them*) I notice your shoes—

SOAPY: Very observant: good for you.

HER: They have holes in them.

SOAPY: Wind pockets. For cross ventilation. (*Does a quick tap step*) One of the multiple privileges of being a rich eccentric.

HER: You? Rich?

SOAPY (*pulls out a fat wallet that he had stuffed with newspaper from the garbage can*): I need a cigar; can you change a hundred.

HIM (*cutting past Her*): Right this way, Sir. (*Hands Soapy a cigar*)

SOAPY (*puts wallet away*): Never mind; put it on my bill. (*Him and Her seat Soapy, making him comfortable*)

HIM and HER:

COMMENT ALLEZ VOUS?
SUCH A PLEASURE SERVING YOU
TRES BIEN, OUI OUI

I'LL BE NICE TO YOU BE NICE TO ME
MERCI

(*Him and Her exit*)

SOAPY (*to audience*):
LEARN A LESSON FROM THE UPPER CRUST
AND TURN YOUR STYLE TO CRUSTY
DON'T CHOW DOWN OR FEED YOUR FACE
WHEN YOU SHOULD SUP
DON'T BE FRIENDLY, JUST BE FUSTY
FROZEN FACES ARE MOST TRUSTY
WHEN YOU'RE LOOKING DOWN AT PEOPLE
DOWN YOUR NOSE FROM OFF THE STEEPLE
WHEN YOU'RE LOOKING DOWN AT PEOPLE
THEY LOOK UP

(*Him and Her enter, put napkin around Soapy's neck and give him a menu*)

HIM and HER:
OUR PLACE IS TO GLIDE WITH GRACE
AND ASSUME THE SOLEMN MANNER OF A
    PARSON
SEE HOW WE CAN GROVEL AND BOW
TO WHOMEVER MAY ENDEAVOR TO YELL

SOAPY:
GARCON!!

HIM (*fawning*): Bonjour, Monsieur—

SOAPY: Whoa there! I'm a wealthy but plain man. I don't use French, hairbrushes or pajamas.

HIM: Oui, Monsieur . . .

SOAPY: You too? Good. You have any soup?

HIM (*sniffing Soapy*): Soap?

SOAPY: Soup!

HIM: Three kinds . . .

SOAPY (*cutting him off*): I'll start with them. Appetizers? (*Him tries to hand Soapy a menu, which he pushes back*) I'm here to eat, not to read. I'll try one of whatever you got. Now what about your main attractions?

HIM: Our Specialties of the House?

SOAPY: Just keep bringin' 'em out; *I'll* tell you what's special.

(*Him and Her load table with dish after covered dish*)

HIM and HER:
     YES, SIR. NO, SIR.
     THE CHICKEN OR THE HAM, WHAT WOULD
        YOU PREFER?
     NO, SIR. YES, SIR.
     THE MARINATED LAMB WITH PEPPERMINT
        LIQUEUR
     AND WHICH WOULD YOU PREFER, THE PASTA
        OR THE CLAM?
     CLEAN YOUR PLATE, IF YOU WILL
     A LA MODE, EAT YOUR FILL
     IF YOU THINK THAT YOU'RE ILL
     WAIT UNTIL YOU SEE YOUR BILL

(*Him and Her exit: Soapy comes down to audience*)

SOAPY:

> DON'T SHOW PLEASURE IN THE FOOD YOU
>   EAT
> OR WINE THE WAITER'S POURING
> CALL IT COLD OR HOT OR SIGH
> "IT'S JUST NOT RIGHT"
> LET 'EM KNOW YOU FIND 'EM BORING
> THEY WILL TURN THEIR MOST ADORING
> IF YOU NEVER CRACK A SMILE
> WITHIN AT LEAST A HALF A MILE OF
> NEVER EVER CRACK A SMILE
> WITHIN THEIR SIGHT

(*Him and Her enter, beckoning Soapy back to the table with new dishes*)

HIM and HER:

> SNAILS IN GARLIC SURE TASTE GREAT
> CATCH THEM BEFORE THEY CRAWL OFF
>   YOUR PLATE
> KEEP ON CARVING, WATCH YOUR WEIGHT
> PEOPLE IN CHINA ARE STARVING

(*Soapy is seated; in a frenzy of activity Him and Her uncover dishes that are now empty; Soapy stretches back as if bloated as Willy passes in front of them*)

WILLY: Four hours, three cooks and seven courses later.

HIM (*exhausted, hands Soapy the bill*): Your bill, Monsieur.

SOAPY (*ripping bill up*): Keep it for kindling. My friend; the minutest coin and I are total strangers.

HIM: Pardon?

SOAPY: Certainly. What I mean to say is that I'm permanently un-financed. (*Him begins shouting in French for Her*) Don't pop your pipes, Pierre. Just get busy, call a cop, and don't keep a gentleman waiting. (*Sits back*)

WILLY (*standing off to the side*): The door slams. There's a crisis in the kitchen.

HER (*rushing to him*): We have a crisis in the kitchen. (*Shoots Willy a disgusted look for stealing her line*)

HIM: What is this?

HER: Our dishwasher looked at all the dishes coming in and quit. (*Him smiles as idea occurs to him; Him and Her look at Soapy, who begins to fidget*)

SOAPY: Why don't I take a walk down to the station and turn myself in? (*Him and Her, one on each side, push Soapy back into his chair*)
> THERE IS JUST ONE WAY, I HATE TO SAY
> THAT I AM LIKE THE DASHING
> THERE IS JUST ONE THING THAT MAKES MY
>   NOGGIN THROB
> I'M NOT FRIGHTENED OF A THRASHING
> OR THE TICKER TAPE A-CRASHING
> OR A TIDAL WAVE A-SPLASHING
> OR A JACK THE RIPPER SLASHING
> OR THE DEVIL'S TEETH A-GNASHING
> BUT MY BLOOD TURNS BLUE
> IT TURNS ICE BLUE
> MY BLOOD TURNS BLUE

IT TURNS ICE BLUE
MY BLOOD TURNS BLUE
AT THE SLIGHTEST PASSING MENTION OF A
    JOB

HIM and HER:

OUR JOB IS TO SERVE THE SNOB
NOT THE NE'ER DO WELL
OUR TASK IS TO DO WHAT THEY ASK
A FROZEN SMILE UPON OUR FACE
A SENSE OF STYLE, A SHOW OF GRACE
FOR THOSE OF YOU WITH MONEY TO BE
    CALLED OUR CLIENTELE
FOR THOSE OF YOU WITH MONEY TO BE
    CALLED OUR CLIENTELE

(*Soapy has tried to escape while they sing; they now collar him*)

SOAPY:

MY BLOOD TURNS BLUE

HIM and HER:

TO THE KITCHEN

SOAPY:

BUT MY BLOOD TURNS BLUE

HIM and HER:

TO THE KITCHEN

SOAPY:

HOW MY BLOOD TURNS BLUE

HIM and HER:

TO THE KITCHEN

SOAPY:

AT THE SLIGHTEST PASSING MENTION OF A
    JOB

(*Him and Her drag a reluctant Soapy out of sight. Willy gestures; lights change to illuminate Jim and Della's apartment*)

WILLY: Turn from the Society Page to the Personal Column. Late Edition: Crosstown at the Dillingham's . . . (*Jim enters, exhausted, taking off his coat; his back is to Della*)

DELLA (*shouts*): Don't move!

JIM (*freezing, shocked*): Thank you, Della. I always like to end a day with heart failure.

DELLA: Close your eyes.

JIM (*closing his eyes*): Are you sneaking a man out the door?

DELLA (*offstage*): All right; now open when I count to three. One . . . (*Pause*)

JIM: Two.

DELLA (*sticks her head in*): I know what comes after one. (*Goes back out*) Two. (*Enters with scraggly Christmas tree branch; a sad specimen of a tree. Della puts tree under Jim's nose*) Three. (*Jim opens his eyes; jumps back in horror*)

JIM: What is it?

DELLA: Our Christmas tree! (*Both look at it with some trepidation*) I found it on Park Avenue, near Eighth, in the gutter.

JIM: What a surprise.

DELLA: I LIKE IT!

JIM: So do I!

DELLA: Just because it's a little low on needles—

JIM: Lots of brown ones.

DELLA: Well, I like him anyway. He has . . . character. Same as you.

JIM: What excellent company. Did you ever notice things have the most character when they don't have anything else?

DELLA: Stop. (*Kisses him*)

JIM: Look at that; his branches just perked up.

DELLA: Did they?

JIM (*kisses her*): I'm sorry about this morning.

DELLA: All forgotten.

JIM: I just . . .

DELLA: All forgotten.

JIM: How was your day?

DELLA: I got more sewing work. Two skirts and a blouse needing mending.

JIM: That's great, Della. It really is.

DELLA (*pauses; unsure of whether to ask him*): How was your day?

JIM (*on edge again*): Same as usual.

DELLA: Oh. (*Cautious*) Did anything look—

JIM (*immediately cuts her off*): No. Not a thing. I would have told you, Della, wouldn't I?

DELLA. Well. Maybe tomorrow.

JIM: Christmas Eve? (*Sarcastic*) I'm sure every store that's open will be hiring dozens of people. (*Pause*) There's nothing out there, Della. Nothing.

DELLA: I know it must be hard.

JIM: You don't know. And you don't know something else; the worst part of it. It isn't getting booted out half the time without them even bothering to look up from their desks to say "No work." It's coming back here, every night, and waiting for you to ask about it.

DELLA (*hurt*): Jim.

JIM: I want to get out of this city, Della. (*Pause*) Maybe it's time we should go home.

DELLA: This is our home now.

JIM: Not if we can't earn enough money to live in it.

DELLA: Is that all you need for a home, Jim? Then why don't we just move into a bank.

JIM: You're not the one they're shutting the door on every day, you know that?

DELLA: Yes, I know that!

JIM: Who will look like the bigger fool when I haven't made anything of myself in this city—

DELLA: We haven't been here long enough.

JIM: How long is "long enough"? Till we starve? Till we don't even have enough money to rent this ugly room? Till we have to beg the train fare to finally get out of here?

DELLA: We are not going anywhere.

JIM: Maybe *you're* not. (*He moves to Della, kisses her neck*) I'm sorry.

DELLA: I'm tired of hearing that.

JIM: I would never leave you, Della. I couldn't.

DELLA: Oh no? Why's that?

JIM: Because every woman I'd see I'd compare to you.

DELLA (*not buying it*): Oh really.

JIM (*trying humor with her*): I'd be walking up to strangers on the street, grabbing their hair and running my fingers through it— (*Does same to her*)

DELLA: Good. I hope you get arrested.

JIM: I'd say, "Nice enough hair you got here; but not half as beautiful as my Della's."

DELLA (*trying not to smile*): Go away.

JIM: It's true.

DELLA (*pulls away*): You are right about one thing, though.

JIM: That's a relief; tell me.

DELLA: It's no wonder this place doesn't look like a home for anyone. Christmas is the day after tomorrow and we don't have a single decoration up.

JIM: We don't have the money for it—

DELLA: Let's not say that awful word once more tonight. Agreed?

JIM: Agreed.

DELLA: Besides, we can make our tree look as proud as the one in Delmonico's without it. All we need is a little imagination.

JIM: You have enough to decorate a forest.

DELLA: We need to help it stand up, for starters—

JIM (*takes nearby can—a strainer—shoves tree in it. It stands*): Done. Now how about decorations?

DELLA: Decorations. (*Exits; re-enters carrying a drawer full of kitchen implements: egg beaters, nutcrackers, etc. Della and Jim hang some on the tree*)

JIM: Very distinctive; I'll say that much for it.

DELLA: We need tinsel or garland.

JIM (*grabs a handful of Della's hair, gently*): Will this do?

DELLA: No!!

JIM (*releases her*): Would snow do? (*Picks up a box of flour or baking soda and sprinkles it over the tree*) Just a few flurries. (*Tosses it up in the air; it comes down on them as well*)

DELLA: That's wonderful!

JIM: He's looking better and better.

DELLA: Oh! We need a star.

JIM: A star, a star. (*Both look around*) I've got it! (*Takes out his pocket watch; hangs it from top of tree*) What do you think?

DELLA: It's lovely.

JIM: Not half bad, is it, Dell? It's got . . .

BOTH (*simultaneously*): Character.

JIM: Now if we only had presents underneath it, too.

SONG: ONCE MORE

JIM and DELLA:
     WHO NEEDS PRESENTS
     BENEATH A TREE

DELLA:

> DO YOU

JIM:

> DO YOU
> DO WE

DELLA:

> IF MISTER CARTIER
> CAME TO ME
> CARRYING A DIAMOND RING
> AND IIE SAID "DELLA DEAR
> TAKE THIS THING," I
> WOULD HAVE TO SAY—

JIM: What?

DELLA:

> WHO NEEDS IT
> WHO WANTS ROCKS UPON THEIR HANDS
> TIIE EXTRA WEIGHT WOULD BE A CHORE
> JUST TELL ME YOU LOVE ME
> ONCE MORE

(*Jim sits Della on his lap*)

JIM:

> IF TEDDY ROOSEVELT
> MARCHED RIGHT IN AND SAT ME
> IN A CHAIR
> AND HE SAID "MISTER D—
> TO YOU FROM ME PLEASE TAKE MY TEDDY
>   BEAR"

DELLA:

> WHO WANTS IT

JIM:

    THOUGH I'D BEG HIM FOR A JOB
    BEFORE I'D SHOW HIM TO THE DOOR
    JUST TELL ME YOU LOVE ME
    ONCE MORE

BOTH:

    EACH DAY WE DEPEND
    ON THREE WORDS AT SUNRISE, OVER AND
       OVER
    ECHOING AT SUNSET ONE COULD GET
       SUSPICIOUS
    HERE WITH MY BEST FRIEND
    ROUTINELY COUNTING BLESSING AFTER
       BLESSING
    IS SO VERY REPE VERY REPETITIOUS
    WILL IT NEVER END

DELLA:

    THE TREASURES PILED HIGH

JIM:

    ONE MORE TIE

DELLA:

    PERSIAN CARPETS ON THE FLOOR

JIM:

    A WHISTLER ON THE WALL

BOTH:

    KEEP THEM ALL
    I CAN GIVE YOU SOMETHING MORE

JIM:

    NOTHING NOVEL

DELLA:

    NOTHING NEW

BOTH:

    JUST ANOTHER
    I LOVE YOU

(*Through following segment, Jim and Della play with the song in mock-operatic seriousness*)

JIM:

> TELL ME YOU LOVE ME
> WHO COULD EVER ASK FOR MORE

DELLA:

> I LOVE YOU I LOVE YOU I LOVE YOU
> TELL ME YOU LOVE ME
> WHO COULD EVER ASK FOR MORE

JIM:

> I LOVE YOU I LOVE YOU

BOTH:

> I LOVE YOU, I LOVE YOU, I LOVE YOU

(*Song is interrupted by a banging on the floor above their heads. They look up*)

CITY IIIM: Quiet down there!

BOTH (*smiling, quietly*):

> SO ALTHOUGII EVERYTHING
> WE HAVE SUNG
> WE HAVE SUNG AND SUNG BEFORE

DELLA:

> BUT MAYBE IF WE SING
> ONCE AGAIN

BOTH:

> I WILL LOVE YOU EVEN MORE

JIM:

> NOTHING NOVEL

DELLA:

> NOTHING NEW

BOTH:

>JUST ANOTHER
>I LOVE YOU

DELLA:

>WHO NEEDS PRESENTS

JIM:

>BENEATH A TREE

DELLA: Maybe just a tiny one? (*Willy appears*)

WILLY: What say we give 'em a little privacy. (*Willy gestures lights down. Jim and Della exit*) It's six A.M.: morning's still wet behind the ears and already the City's got its hands full. (*City Him and Her rush in, dressed in cooking aprons; throw Soapy Smith from stage. He sits by garbage can*)

HIM: Don't you ever set foot in here again, Mac, not if you know what's good for you.

SOAPY (*exhausted, pleading*): I know what's good for me. Calling a policeman would be good for me. Jail would be the best thing that ever happened to me.

HER (*to him*): He's addled, don't you see? It's Christmas Eve. Why don't we let the poor man go.

SOAPY: What?

HIM: Maybe you're right.

SOAPY: She's wrong, she's wrong!!

HER: Merry Christmas to ya, pal. You want me to wrap up a lunch for ya?

SOAPY: Lunch! (*Sinks back, holding his stomach*) Pleez, go away.

HER (*looking up*): If only it would snow! (*Him and Her exit*)

SOAPY: The black-hearted tarantulas; they have no respect for the law. (*Jim enters from the audience; he is angry, reading the paper. Sees Willy*)

JIM: Nothing again, Willy.

WILLY: Slim pickings this time of year, Mr. D. But after the holidays, just you wait and see.

JIM: I'm still waiting, Willy. But I can't say for how long. (*Jim hears a moaning sound coming from Soapy; sees him and goes to his side*) Are you all right?

SOAPY: Not in the least, but I might digest better right side up. (*Gestures to be helped up; Jim does*) Thank you kindly. Your assistance comes in handier than a powder rag at a fat man's ball.

JIM: What happened to you?

SOAPY: Injustice happened to me. Even worse, charity. Every culinary establishment in this city has its knife and fork into me.

JIM: You need something to eat?

SOAPY (*holds stomach, cringes*): Bite your tongue. I've just finished my fifth breakfast since dawn; I'm a walking smorgasboard.

JIM: You must have been hungry.

SOAPY: Hunger has nothing to do with it! This is pure gumption, believe you me. I have never worked harder in my life. These cafe owners are criminals: I have stiffed each and every bill and not one has had the common decency to call the coppers.

JIM: You *want* to be arrested?

SOAPY: With all my heart. It is high time to flee this city, my friend. Winter is most inhospitable to gentlemen of leisure.

JIM: I'll say. (*Jim crosses dejectedly to bench*)

SOAPY (*looking Jim over*): Do I detect a similar odor of despondency in your tone, Sir?

JIM (*smiles*): Well, let's just say that lately I've had a run of bum luck.

SOAPY (*winces*): You don't mean that.

JIM: Bum luck? Sure I do. (*Jim begins to start out*)

SOAPY: Good heavens, man. You are laboring under a prejudical misapprehension. (*Jim shrugs; begins to walk away; Soapy takes his arm*)

SONG: BUM LUCK

SOAPY:

    SAY MISTER CAN YOU SPARE THE TIME TO
    HEAR ME HAVE MY SAY

'CAUSE IT PAINS MY TICKER DEEPLY WHEN I
    HEAR YOU TALK THAT WAY
AS A JOE WHO LIVES BY WITS ALONE,
    AVOIDING EVERY TRAP
THERE'S NO BETTER GUY TO TELL YOU THAT
    A BUM
GETS ONE BUM RAP

IF A FELLA'S LEG FEELS LIKE IT'S LEAD

JIM:

It's a bum leg?

SOAPY:

How right you are.
IF YOU LOSE YOUR SHIRT WHEN YOUR
    HORSE DROPS
DEAD—

JIM:

It's a bum tip?

SOAPY:

Tell me about it.
BUT MY MEALS ARE FREE WHICH INCLUDES
    FREE LUNCH
IT'S A BIG PARK BENCH SO THERE AIN'T NO
    CRUNCH
I DON'T GOT NO CLOCK OR A BOSS TO PUNCH
SO IF THAT'S BUM LUCK
I'M A LUCKY GUY
BUM BUM BUM BE-BUM BE-BUM BUM LUCK
BUM BUM BUM BE-BUM BE-BUM BUM LUCK

BOTH:

BUM BUM BUM BE-BUM BE-BUM BUM LUCK
BUM BUM BUM BE-BUM BE-BUM BUM LUCK

(*Soapy and Jim cross to the garbage can. Soapy pulls out a beat-up straw hat and muffler and dresses Jim up as a bum. They sit on edge of stage*)

SOAPY:

> HEY

JIM:

> HEY

SOAPY:

> HO

JIM:

> HO

SOAPY:

> IF YOU LACK A PENSION
> I FEEL THAT I MUST MENTION
> THE LUCKIEST INVENTION
> EVER KNOWN TO MAN

BOTH:

> IS THE GARBAGE CAN

SOAPY:

> YES RIGHT

JIM:

> RIGHT

SOAPY:

> HERE

JIM:

> HERE

BOTH:

> FOR YOUR RESTITUTION
> FULL OF CONTRIBUTION FROM THE MASSES
> NOW AND THEN THERE'S ONE OR TWO THAT
>   PASSES BY
> AND WHAT TO THEM IS ONLY JUNK

JIM:

    IS USED

SOAPY:

    OR RIPPED

BOTH:

    OR MAYBE SHRUNK
    THEY DROP IT LIKE A GIFT
    FOR THOSE OF US WHO DRIFT
    YES I COULD FILL A TRUNK
    THAT WOULD BREAK YOUR BACK TO LIFT
    FROM THE FORTUNE LEFT BEHIND BY MAN
    IN A GARBAGE CAN

(Brief dance break. Jim is caught up completely in Soapy's exuberance)

    BUM BUM BUM BE-BUM BE-BUM BUM LUCK
    BUM BUM BUM BE-BUM BE-BUM BUM LUCK

JIM:

    THERE'S GIVERS

SOAPY:

    AND THERE'S TAKERS

BOTH:

    AND THE TWAIN DON'T EVER MEET
    EXCEPT WHEN ONE IS GIVING TO A TAKER
    ON THE STREET

SOAPY:

    BUT IF TAKERS STOPPED THEIR TAKING

JIM:

    HOW WOULD GIVERS FEEL INSIDE

BOTH:

    IT'S OUR MORAL OBLIGATION TO KEEP
    GIVING GIVERS PRIDE

SOAPY:

IF YOU BUY A BRIDGE 'CAUSE THE DEAL'S SO
HOT

JIM:

IT'S A BUM DEAL

SOAPY:

Couldn't be worse. IF A COW DON'T GIVE YOU
ALL THAT IT'S GOT

JIM:

IT'S A . . .

SOAPY:

BUM STEER

JIM:

You're a genius.

SOAPY:

I know.

BOTH:

BUT I DON'T PAY RENT 'CAUSE THE WORLD IS
FREE
LAUGH A LOT AT BAD TIMES AND THEY FLEE
AND I LET MY LIFE TAKE CARE OF ME

SOAPY:

SO IF THAT'S BUM LUCK

JIM:

YES, IF THAT'S BUM LUCK

SOAPY:

GIVE ME MORE BUM LUCK

BOTH:

'CAUSE I'M A LUCKY GUY

(*Soapy and Jim work their way back to the bench and sit*)

JIM:

BUM BUM BUM BE-BUM BE-BUM BUM LUCK
BUM BUM BUM BE-BUM BE-BUM LUCKY GUY

Leslie Hicks (*left*) as Della with Jeff McCarthy as Jim
in the original 1984 production.

All photos of Lamb's Theatre Company productions by Carol Rosegg.

Eddie Korbich as Willy in the 1992 production.

Lou Williford (*left*) as The City: Her with Michael Farina as The City: Him
in the 1992 production.

(*Sitting, left to right*): Jessica Beltz and Scott Waara; (*standing, left to right*)
Michael Calkins, Adam Bryant, Gabriel Barre and Rebecca Renfroe
in the 1988 production.

SOAPY:

> BUM BUM BUM BE-BUM BE-BUM BUM LUCK
> BUM BUM BUM BE-BUM BE-BUM

BOTH:

> I'M A LUCKY GUY

SOAPY: Now you're learning. (*Song concludes*)

SOAPY (*putting out hand*): Soapy Smith.

JIM (*shaking hand*): Jim Dillingham. Pleased to meet you, Soapy, but I'd better be moving on.

SOAPY: Moving on is just what I had in mind, Jim Dillingham. It is my chosen vocation, and the perfect time to practice my craft.

JIM: Is it?

SOAPY (*walks with Jim arm in arm*): Most assuredly. When wild geese honk high of nights, and women without scalskin coats grow kind to their husbands, it is high time to take to the road. What would you say to the two of us moving on together?

JIM (*surprised*): To where?

SOAPY: Warmer climes and hot pebbled beaches: To Florida, or Venezuela, whichever's closer by coach. We can travel first class, like the movers and shakers of this moved and shaken city.

JIM: How do you figure we can do that?

SOAPY: You can sell your watch.

JIM: My watch? (*Reaches into his pocket, panics, realizing it is gone*) MY WATCH!

SOAPY (*takes Jim's watch out of his own pocket*): Precisely, Jim Dillingham. I think it should fetch us any number of one-way tickets.

JIM: Thanks for asking me to go, Soapy, But I can't.

SOAPY: Why so?

JIM: I'm married.

SOAPY: More's the reason.

JIM: You don't understand.

SOAPY: Are you happy with your life at present, Jim Dillingham?

JIM (*pause*): No—

SOAPY: Then six-to-one odds your wife's unhappy, too. Come away, move away, give the woman a vacation.

JIM: I don't think so, Soapy. (*Takes watch back*)

SOAPY: This Mrs. must be mighty special, femininely speaking.

JIM: She is.

SOAPY: Pretty, too, to ice 'he cake?

JIM: More beautiful than you could imagine.

SOAPY: Give me a moment! (*Puts hand to head*) Big brown eyes—

JIM: Blue—

SOAPY: Long blond hair—

JIM: Halfway down her back.

SOAPY (*opens his eyes, a recognition*): Is the Mrs. about so high, with a smile so bright it hurts?

JIM (*smiles*): That's Della.

SOAPY: I know of whom you speak; I have seen such a damsel in the neighborhood. Jim Dillingham, you are a lucky bum. That woman's pretty enough to make an anchovy forget his vows. (*Sighs*) Well then, I must seek domestic quarters. Back to work.

JIM: Work?

SOAPY: Observe. (*Takes a rock out of garbage*) A projectile. Are you watching?

JIM: I'm watching.

SOAPY: Keep your eyes on the ball. (*Winds up; tosses it offstage. Sound of loud crash, and a yelp*) It's a home run!

JIM: What did you do that for?

SOAPY: A blow for justice. And you, my friend, are a witness. (*City Him, dressed as a policeman, runs in. Soapy stands by, hands in pockets, beaming expectantly*)

HIM (*to Jim*): Who threw that?

SOAPY: Don't you figure that I might have had something to do with it?

HIM: And still be standing here? (*Looking about*) Don't be a wise apple.

JIM: But Officer, he did!

SOAPY (*indignant; to Him*): Good Lord, Sir, you aren't dealing with an all-star one-night theatrical.

JIM: He picked up a stone, wound up and tossed it—

HIM: That's enough out of you. (*Looks down the block*) You there! (*Blows whistle*) Yes, you—on the curb. Hold your horses, you're under arrest! WAIT, I SAID! (*Runs off*) STOP IN THE NAME OF THE LAW!

SOAPY (*after an astonished look at Jim, he bolts after the policeman*): Police! POLICE! CALL OUT MY PADDY WAGON! (*Runs off. Jim shakes his head, bemused, then looks around him, tucking in his coat as musical underscoring begins. He takes a reluctant look at his newspaper, tucks it under his arm and exits. Willy enters and sits on the park bench, addressing the audience*)

WILLY: Afternoon edition: Christmas, a dozen hours away, and the City too crowded for anyone to take a deep breath. (*City Him and Her enter as they speak*)

HER: Mobs and masses—

HIM: Every pavement packed—

WILLY: Folks from all over—

HER: Coming from all ways—

HIM: The Pennsylvania Railroad—

HER: Heavy walking shoes.

HIM: Ellis Island.

HER: The Stork—

HIM: Auto—

HER: Or thumb—

WILLY: For all things—

HIM: Art schools—

HER: Fresh fish and vegetables—

HIM: The Annual Dressmaker's Convention—

HER: Pots of Gold—

HIM: Initialed—

HER: Melted—

HIM: Exploration—

HER: Education—

HIM: Assimilation—

HER: The Stage—

HIM and HER: Ambition—(*Jim and Della enter and freeze as Willy speaks. Him and Her change into the costumes of salespeople. All actors speak directly to audience*)

WILLY: All these audition for the population. But this City's mighty selective. Every man who sets foot on the stones of Manhattan has got to fight. Fight at once until he or the other guy wins. And there's no resting between rounds, because there are no rounds. It's a slugfest from the first, a fight to the finish. Your opponent is the City—

HIM (*facing audience, though he is addressing Della*): Yes?

HER (*facing audience, though she is addressing Jim*): You'd like something?

WILLY: You do battle with it from the first time the ferry boat lands until it's either yours or it's conquered you.

JIM (*crosses to City Her*): Could you tell me how much that set in front of your glass case costs?

HER: Only nineteen dollars and forty-seven cents.

JIM (*taken aback*): Nineteen dollars and forty-seven cents?

WILLY: And oh, the city is a general in the ring. Not only by blows does it seek to subdue you. It woos you to its heart with the sublety of a siren—

HIM (*to Della*): Quite distinguished, isn't it? (*Gestures to imaginary object before the audience*)

DELLA (*crosses to City Him*): Oh yes.

HIM: And a mere twenty-three dollars and ten cents.

DELLA (*swallows*): Is that all?

WILLY: The City is a combination of Delilah, green chartreuse, Beethoven, a frosty glass of beer and John L. Sullivan—on his best day.

HIM and HER: That's our sale price.

WILLY (*chuckles*): Sales around the holidays are grand things; shows the shopkeepers still have a sense of humor.

JIM: It's Christmas Eve; don't you think you could be lowering your price a little?

HER: *Lowering?* We sell only quality merchandise, Sir. For customers of quality. The sort that don't quibble about pennies.

HIM (*to Della*): I don't see any point to taking it out of our window if you're not really serious about it.

DELLA: I am serious . . . but it's such a lot of money.

HIM (*sniffs*): To some. Excuse me, Madam. But there are *customers* waiting. If you're simply here to window shop you could best do it from the sidewalk. (*Jim and Della walk out. Him and Her turn to imaginary customers as Willy steps between them, whispering as if a spirit of Christmas*)

WILLY: Merry Christmas—

HIM (*to imaginary customer*): That will be thirty-two fifteen. Unless you'd like the true top of the line; let me show you something much nicer—

WILLY (*to Her*): Season's greetings—

HER (*to imaginary customer*): Gift wrap is extra, of course. (*Eyebrows up*) You want bows, *too?*

WILLY: There's something else that grows round the holidays; something with roots stronger than holly or mistletoe—

HIM (*counting out money that he's taken from his pocket*): What a rewarding season—

WILLY: The kind of growth that gets its roots so deep you can't blast or burn them out—

HER (*counting her money*): Such a bundle of Christmas spirit—

WILLY: It's the underbelly to a Christmas present; a price tag with teeth and an appetite.

HIM (*to Her*): Would you like help counting? (*She hides her money quickly*)

WILLY (*moving off*): It's called . . . (*whispers*) Greed.

HIM and HER (*welcoming it*): GREED!

SONG: GREED

HIM:

GREED IS THE COLOR DARKER THAN BLACK

HER:

A SACKFUL OF NEED, TAKE THE NEED THEN
TAKE THE SACK
AND IF YOU FEEL THE GUILT FROM THE
MILK THAT YOU SPILT
YOU LACK GREED

TAKE WHAT YOU HAVE TO, DON'T THINK
TWICE
HARD ON THE MAKE, YOU AWAKE IN
PARADISE
IN THE END A MEANS TO THE END JUSTIFIES
THE MEANS FOR GREED

HIM:

GREED IS HANDSOME
GREED IS WRONG
I FEEL GREEDY ALL DAY LONG

HER:

LIKE A FIRE
GREED CAN BURN
BURNING DESIRE MY CONCERN

BOTH:

BLEED WHO YOU HAVE TO, DON'T PLAY
GOOD
DO THE DIRTY DEED, INDEED YOU SHOULD
NEVER LOOK BACK, HAVE A HEART THAT IS
BLACKER THAN GREED

HIM:

I WOULD LIKE TO TAKE YOUR MONEY

HER:

> I WOULD LIKE TO SPEND IT

BOTH:

> IF YOUR DAY TO NOW'S BEEN SUNNY
> WE WOULD LIKE TO END IT
> TAKING FOLKS'S HARD EARNED LOOT
> CAN BE SO VERY FINE

HIM:

> SHE WILL KICK YOUR OL' PATOOT

HER:

> SLAP YOUR FACE AND STOMP YOUR BOOT

HIM:

> WHILE PERFECTLY I EXECUTE

BOTH:

> THE PINCHING OF YOUR POCKETS ONE BY
>   ONE
>
> ONE BY ONE WE COME TO KNOW
> THE LOVE OF MONEY'S GOLDEN GLOW
> LITTLE BY LITTLE WE ALL TUNE OUR
>   FIDDLE
> TO MACHIAVELLIAN, ANGEL OR HELLION
> SOONER OR LATER WE ALL GOTTA CATER
> TO GREED

(*Jim and Della appear*)

DELLA:

> WHAT GOOD IS A HOLIDAY
> WHEN A DOLLAR NINETY-SEVEN IS WHAT
>   YOU'VE GOT
> NO A DOLLAR NINETY-SEVEN IS NOT A LOT
> TO SPEND ON HIM.
> MY JIM

DELLA:

WHAT GOOD IS A
  HOLIDAY
WHEN A DOLLAR
  NINETY-SEVEN

IS ALL YOU'VE GOT

NO A DOLLAR
  NINETY-SEVEN

IS NOT A LOT

A HOLIDAY'S A
  WASTE OF TIME

JIM:

WHAT GOOD IS A
  HOLIDAY

WHEN YOU HAVEN'T
  GOT A PENNY

I'D RATHER THAT
  THERE WEREN'T
  ANY

WHEN YOU HAVEN'T
  GOT A DIME

A HOLIDAY'S A
  WASTE OF TIME

(Jim and Della move together)

JIM and DELLA:

HAVE YOU SEEN THE LOOK IN THE EYES OF
  THE CLERK
IN THE SHOP ON THE CORNER OF THE
  STREET

HIM and HER:

GREED! *(Him and Her inch their way upstage)*

JIM and DELLA:

STARING LIKE A CROOK IN DISGUISE HARD
  AT WORK

IN THE SHOP EXTRACTING ALL YOUR
    WAGES
WHY IT COSTS AN ARM AND A LEG JUST TO
    LOOK
IN THE SHOP ON THE CORNER OF THE
    STREET

HIM and HER:
GREED!

JIM and DELLA:
WHAT WOULD BE THE HARM IF WE BEG FOR
    A LOOK
AT THE BOOK IN THE SHOP ON THE CORNER
    OF THE STREET
WITH THE PICTURES ON THE PAGES

HIM: You would like a catalogue?

DELLA: Uh, how much?

HIM: Free!

DELLA: Good!

HIM: —With a ten dollar purchase. (*All change places with a circular, merry-go-round pattern*)

HIM and HER:	JIM and DELLA:
GREED IS THE	WHAT GOOD IS
COLOR DARKER	A HOLIDAY . . .
THAN BLACK	
WE WOULD LIKE TO	
TAKE	
YOUR MONEY	

WE WOULD LIKE TO
  SPEND IT
IF YOUR DAY TO
  NOW'S BEEN
  SUNNY
WE WOULD LIKE TO
  END IT
WE WILL GLADLY
  PINCH YOUR
  POCKETS ONE BY
  ONE
A HOLIDAY'S A LOT
  OF FUN
(*Chanted*) GREED,
  GREED. GREED,
  GREED. . . .

JIM and DELLA:

    NOTICE HOW THEIR TEETH SEEM TO GRIND
      AT THE SHOW
    OR THE FLASH OF A LITTLE BIT OF GREEN
    NOTHING IS BENEATH HUMANKIND WHEN
      THEY KNOW
    THERE IS CASH TO FATTEN UP A POCKET
    EVEN VERY RICH PEOPLE ITCH AT THE
      SIGHT
    OR THE FLASH OF A LITTLE BIT OF GREEN
    DOESN'T MATTER WHICH, POOR OR RICH,
      WRONG OR RIGHT

ALL:

    EVERYBODY HAS A POCKET FULL OF
      GREED—

HIM and HER:

>GREED IS THE MUSIC I HAVE FOUND
>THE JINGLE OF GREED IS A GREEDY SOUND
>DEAFENS MY EARS, LET'S HEAR THREE
>   CHEERS
>FOR GREED HIP HIP HOORAY HIP HIP
>   HOORAY HIP HIP HOORAY

HIM:

>GREED IS PLEASURE
>FOR AWHILE
>GREED WE MEASURE
>BY THE MILE

HER:

>GREED IS LONELY
>GREED IS JAILS
>GREED IS ONLY
>COFFIN NAILS

HIM and HER:

>GREED IS A COLOR DARKER THAN PAIN
>GROWS LIKE A WEED AND LEAVES A GREEDY
>   STAIN
>GREED HARD AS TEAK, BUT NO MATTER I AM
>   WEAK
>FROM GREED, HA GREED BOO GREED
>
>HA, HA, HA, HA
>GREED

ALL:

>EVERYBODY HAS A POCKET FULL OF GREED

(*All exit except for Willy*)

WILLY: Almost time to close up shop. And time for last minute shopping for those with coins still left in their pockets . . . (*Jim and Della enter. They watch Him and Her carry huge bundles of presents)* . . . Or those that don't.

HER *(talking to Him)*: Oh, no. I finished shopping for my husband weeks ago. These are for the help.

HER: I didn't know what to get my wife, so I got her *everything.* *(Him and Her exit, laughing. Willy walks behind Della, speaking softly)*

WILLY *(to Della)*: A dollar ninety-seven did you say, Mrs. Dillingham? And how far did that take you? *(Willy moves behind Jim)* She doesn't need a Christmas present, Mr. D. She said so herself. "Madame Sofronie's Hair Goods of All Kinds." *(Della touches her hand to her hair; Her enters as Madame Sofronie)* "Varrelman and Clark, Procurers of Employment"—*(Willy holds a flyer up in his hand; Jim approaches, takes it as if ripping it down from a wall, looks at it. City Him enters as employment clerk, carrying clipboard)*

SONG: POCKETS

WILLY:

> POCKETS
> NOTHING IN MY POCKETS
> NOTHING UP MY SLEEVE
> I WON'T VENTURE TO DECEIVE YOU
> BELIEVE ME
> WHAT I HAVE TO SAY IS SIMPLE
> HOW CAN PEOPLE BE SO SIMPLE
> DON'T THEY KNOW THE WORLD IS ROUGH
> NEVER SEEMS TO BE ENOUGH
> OF THE STUFF CALLED LOVE

JUST A BUNCH OF LONELY HANDS
IN A BUNCH OF EMPTY POCKETS

DELLA (*approaches Madame Sofronie*): Will you buy my hair?

HER: I buy hair. Take off yer scarf and let's have a sight at the looks of it. (*Her and Della freeze; Jim walks to clerk*)

JIM: I saw the handbill—it says you're hiring—

HIM: We're hiring. It's railroad work. You ready to travel?

JIM: Travel? (*Jim and he freeze*)

WILLY:

MIDNIGHT
HEAR THE CLOCK CHIME
WAKE UP
TIME TO GO TO WORK
WORK HARD
FOR A NICKEL OR A DIME
EVERY DAY OF YOUR LIFE
UNTIL SOMETIME
YOU WILL HEAR A CLOCK CHIME
WHEN THE REAPER KNOCKS
AND IT'S YOUR TIME
ON YOU LIKE A FOX
SOMEHOW FROM THE DARK
SECRETLY AT MIDNIGHT

CHILDREN
ALWAYS THERE ARE CHILDREN
TOUCHING IN THE DARK
SCRATCHING HEARTS UPON THE BARK

OF A TREE IN THE PARK
DID YOU EVER SEE THEIR FACES
SILLY GRINS UPON THEIR FACES
SEVENTEEN TO NINETY-FIVE
DON'T KNOW HOW THEY ALL SURVIVE
THIS CONNIVING WORLD
BUT WHAT A LOT OF LOVELY EYES
ON THE FACES OF THE CHILDREN

HER (*to Della, lifting her hair*): Twenty dollars.

DELLA (*pause*): Cut it quickly. (*They exit. Soapy is seen in dim light behind Jim and Him*)

SOAPY: Then it's six-to-one odds that your wife's unhappy, too. Come away, move away; give the woman a vacation.

HIM (*to Jim*): You interested or not?

JIM: I'm thinking.

HIM: Think quick, Mister. And step aside—let the fellas behind you up to the window.

WILLY:

MIDNIGHT
HEAR THE CLOCK CHIME
NEW DAY
TIME TO GO TO WORK
WORK HARD
FIND A LADDER HAVE A CLIMB
EVERY DAY OF YOUR LIFE
UNTIL SOMETIME
YOU WILL HEAR A CLOCK CHIME

TIME TO BE THE KING
YES IT'S YOUR TIME
WHAT A FUNNY THING
ALWAYS IN THE WORLD
SOMEWHERE IT IS MIDNIGHT

(Jim and Him exit. We see in silhouette on curtain Della's hair being cut. Lights go down. Willy is pinspotted at center)

MORNING
DON'T YOU LOVE THE MORNING
NOTHING IS SO BRIGHT
THAT IS WHY I MUST INVITE YOU
TO SHARE ITS LIGHT
NO THERE'S NOTHING IN MY POCKETS
ARE YOUR HANDS STILL IN YOUR POCKETS
THERE IS NOT A WORTHY THING
IN THE POCKETS OF A KING
NOT A RING OR GEM
THAT CAN WARM THEM
LIKE ANOTHER LOVING HAND
ON A BRIGHT AND SHINY MORNING
IF YOU TAKE ME BY THE HAND
I WILL BRING YOU TO THE MORNING
FOLLOW ME TO MORNING
COME INTO THE MORNING
FOLLOW ME, COME ALONG
I'M ON MY WAY
I'M ON MY WAY
FOLLOW ME COME ALONG TO THE MORNING
I'M ON MY WAY
I'M ON MY WAY

(*At song's conclusion, Willy looks up into the dark night sky, blinks; a star twinkles. Blackout. Lights rise to reveal Soapy Smith pacing in a circle on an empty stage*)

SOAPY: Desperate times call for desperate decisions . . . (*Him enters, carrying an umbrella. Soapy spots him*) . . . and this is one desperate bum. (*Soapy runs up to him, grabs his umbrella; twirls it before him with deliberate braggadocio*)

HIM: That's my umbrella!

SOAPY (*sneering*): Is it, now? Well, why don't you call a policeman? I *took* your umbrella. Now it's my umbrella. Call a cop, there's one standing right there on the next corner—

HIM: Ah-well-that is-you know how these mistakes occur . . .

SOAPY: Mistakes? There is no mistake. I pinched your umbrella. (*Grabs him by the arm*) Come on now; hand me over—(*Begins to drag him offstage*)

HIM (*stopping*): I-ah-if it's your umbrella I hope you'll excuse me. I picked it up this morning in a restaurant. I know I shouldn't have, but, ah . . . if you recognize it as yours I hope you'll forgive me. (*Backing off*) Merry Christmas! (*Runs off*)

SOAPY (*clasps hands over eyes*): I am cursed by good fortune. (*Tosses umbrella offstage. Her enters chewing gum, swinging hips exaggeratedly, looking at imaginary store window. Soapy spots her; looks to audience*)—But behind every cloud is a silver lining— (*Him reenters, dressed as policeman. He stands there, twirling his club*)—Or a brass one at least. (*Soapy approaches her as sleazy masher*) Heh heh heh. Hello there, Bedelia. Don't you want to come and play in my yard. (*Looks at the policeman, who ignores him. Soapy raises his voice*) Or can I come romp in your garden, my little tomato—you are looking full of juice and ripe for the picking. (*Soapy slides his arm around her*) And do I like the looks of those stems! (*She looks; policeman has looked away and exits. Soapy does not see his exit*)

HER: Sure, Bud. If you'll blow me to a pail of suds. I'd have spoken to you sooner but the cop was watching. (*She grabs Soapy's arm. Soapy, stunned, looks for cop, now gone*) Hey! What kind of guy are you, anyways? What we need is some snow. (*Exits*)

SONG: *BUM LUCK (REPRISE)*

SOAPY:

> SO YOU WEAR A SMILE AND YOU DON'T
>   COMPLAIN
> EVERY STROKE OF LUCK IS A STROKE OF
>   PAIN
> AND YOU HOPE THAT SUN'S GONNA TURN TO
>   RAIN
>
> SO IF THAT'S BUM LUCK
> I'M A LUCKY
>
> BUM BUM BUM BUM BUM BUM BUM BUM
>   LUCK
> BUM BUM BUM BE-BUM BE-BUM BUM

(*Soapy exits*)

WILLY: Later Christmas Eve, by the light of the stars, Della returns home to await her Jim. (*Della enters, her hair has been shorn*)

SONG: THE SAME GIRL

DELLA:

AM I STILL THE SAME GIRL
OR AM I SOMEONE HE WON'T KNOW
SHOULD I CHANGE MY NAME
ONE TO GO WITH MY LOOK
OR MY LACK THEREOF
AM I STILL THE SAME GIRL
HE TOOK
TO LOVE

AND THOUGH I'M KIND OF NERVOUS
AND THOUGH I HAVE THE BUTTERFLIES
I CAN'T WAIT TO SEE HIM SEE HIS NEW
   SURPRISE

CLOSE YOUR EYES, JIM
DON'T LOOK YET PLEASE
CLOSE THEM TIGHT
DON'T YOU PEEK
COUNT OF THREE
NOT ONE LOOK
TILL I SAY
ONE-TWO-THREE AND MERRY CHRISTMAS I
   LOVE YOU
THAT I DO MY JIM
MY JIM
STILL I WONDER IF HE'LL BE
THE SAME SWEET MAN IN LOVE WITH ME

MAYBE HE WILL THINK THAT I'M PRETTY AS
   A PICTURE

A NEW EXPERIENCE, ADORABLE
MAYBE HE WILL THINK THAT I'M
    UNAPPEALING
DULL AND PLAINLY HORRIBLE
OH WHERE CAN I HIDE CAN I
WHERE CAN I HIDE
MAYBE I WILL DISAPPEAR
RUN AWAY TO SIAM
WHERE NO ONE KNOWS WHO I AM
AND NO ONE EVEN KNOWS I'M HERE

YES I FELL AND HIT MY HEAD
AND NOW I'M LYING IN A STRANGE DOUBLE
    BED
AND I'M STARING UP AT TWO DOUBLE CHINS
OF THESE BROKEN-HEARTED SIAMESE
    TWINS
YES, ONE BROKEN HEART
BUT TWO FUNNY GRINS
AND THEY'VE TAKEN ME FOR DEAD
UNTIL I POPPED AWAKE AND SAID
"HELLO, I'M DELLA"
AND THEY SAID, "NO YOU'RE NOT"
SO I SAID, "LISTEN FELLA"
AND THEY SAID, "LISTEN TO WHAT?"
THEY SAID, "DELLA HAS LOCKS THAT FLOW
DOWN BELOW HER WAIST THEY GO
AND YOU HAVE A MOP THAT FLOPS
FROM THE TOP OF YOUR HEAD THEN STOPS"
NEVER BEEN TO SIAM. HOW CAN SOMEONE
    DISAPPEAR
I AM ONLY RIGHT HERE
WONDERING WHO I AM

AM I STILL THE SAME GIRL
WAITING WITH THE BUTTERFLIES
I CAN'T WAIT TO SEE HIM SEE HIS NEW
   SURPRISE

CLOSE YOUR EYES, JIM
DON'T LOOK THAT WAY
PLEASE DON'T STARE
YES I DID
I CUT MY HAIR
YOU WILL SEE
BEFORE YOU KNOW IT
ONE-TWO-THREE I'M BEAUTIFUL AND I LOVE
   YOU
THAT I DO MY JIM
MY JIM
STILL I WONDER IF HE'LL BE
THE SAME SWEET MAN IN LOVE WITH ME

(Jim has entered by conclusion of song; he stares at Della as music stops. There is a long pause. Except for Jim and Della, the stage is empty. It is a scene to be played with little movement and only essential props)

DELLA: Jim: don't look at me that way. I had my hair cut off and sold it because I couldn't have lived through Christmas without giving you a present. It will grow again. It will, Jim. You won't mind, will you? I just had to do it. My hair grows awfully fast, just wait. *(Pause)* Say Merry Christmas, Jim, and let's be happy. You don't know what a gift, what a wonderful, special gift I've gotten for you.

JIM *(pause. Stunned)*: You cut off your hair.

DELLA: Yes! I had to—to sell it. Don't you like me just as well, anyhow? Jim? I'm me without my hair, aren't I?

JIM: You say . . . your hair is gone.

DELLA: You needn't look for it. It's sold, I told you. I sold it for you Jim! IT'S ALL I HAD AND NOW I DON'T HAVE ANYTHING. (*Cries; Jim goes to her, hugs her*)

JIM: Of course you do. Don't get me wrong, Della. Don't. There's nothing in the world, nothing in the way of a haircut or a shampoo or a shave that could change my mind about you. But if you unwrap this I think you'll see why you had me going for awhile. (*Jim takes from his pocket a wrapped present*)

DELLA: Oh, Jim! A present! For me. You shouldn't have. How could you . . . Wait. Open yours first. (*Exits, comes back quickly with Jim's present; hands it to him*)

JIM: No, Dell. You go first.

DELLA: You. Unwrap it. I can't wait.

JIM: Right after you look at yours—

DELLA: You first—

JIM: Della, unwrap your present!

WILLY: This went on for some time.

JIM: Together, then. (*Both unwrap as music begins to play underneath*)

DELLA (*opens hers first, taking out combs*): Oh, Jim. Combs! They're perfection! How did you know I always wanted these?

JIM: I saw you looking. (*Proudly*) Pure tortoise shell.

DELLA: They're so wonderful! (*Realizes hair is gone; immediately sobs*) This is the most wonderful present anyone could ever get.

JIM (*holding her*): Come on now, Dell. Don't worry. Your hair will grow back; you said so yourself.

DELLA: It will, won't it?

JIM: Of course it will. Like a weed. (*Della shoots him a look*) A beautiful weed!

DELLA: Open your present, Jim. (*Tries to smile*) Do it now. (*Jim opens present; his face falls*)

JIM (*emotionless*): A watch fob.

DELLA: Yes!

JIM: A watch fob.

DELLA: Jim; don't you like it?

JIM: Della, this is the most elegant present I have gotten in my entire life. It is the best. Just like you. (*Kisses her*)

DELLA: Isn't it a dandy, Jim?

JIM: It is.

DELLA: I hunted all over town to find it. You'll have to look at your watch a hundred times a day. Give me your watch; I want to see how it looks on it.

JIM: Not now, Dell—

DELLA: Yes, now. It won't take a minute.

JIM: Let's put our Christmas gifts away and keep 'em awhile. They're just too nice to use right now.

WILLY (*observing; speaks to audience*): The Magi were wise men, wonderfully wise men who brought gifts to the Babe in the manger. They invented the art of giving Christmas gifts. Being wise, their gifts were no doubt wise ones—

DELLA: Jim; why don't you put it on your watch?

JIM (*pause*): I sold the watch to get money to buy your combs.

WILLY: And here I have related to you the chronicle of two foolish children in a flat who most unwisely sacrificed for each other the greatest treasures of their house.

DELLA: Not your great-grandfather's watch! You didn't!

JIM: I did. And I'd do it again.

DELLA: But that's your family treasure—

JIM: I've got a richer one. I turned down a job today.

DELLA: But why?

JIM: Because it would mean going away. And there's no way I'm leaving you. Ever.

WILLY: But in the last word to the wise of these days; let it be said that of all who give gifts, these two were the wisest. Of all who give and receive gifts, such as they are the wisest. Everywhere, they are the wisest. They are the Magi.

JIM: I love you, Della.

DELLA: And I love you, Jim Dillingham.

SONG: *THE GIFT OF CHRISTMAS*

WILLY:
>
> THREE WISE KINGS WATCH A SHINING STAR
> TRAV'LING FAR WITH THEIR GOLD AND
>   TREASURE
> THREE WISE KINGS AND A VOICE THAT
>   SINGS
> OF THE GIFT OF CHRISTMAS
>
> THREE WISE KINGS
>   HEAR A BABY CRY
> STAR ON HIGH
>   LIGHTS A DISTANT STABLE
> THREE WISE KINGS
>   AND A VOICE THAT SINGS
> OF THE GIFTS OF CHRISTMAS

WILLY:

THREE WISE KINGS	HIM, HER, JIM, DELLA:
WATCH A BABY	BUM, BUM, BUM . . .
SMILE	

NOT BEGUILED
BY THEIR GOLD AND
   TREASURE
NOT BY THINGS
BUT THE LOVE ONE
   BRINGS

COMES THE GIFT OF CHRISTMAS

SOAPY: Will you listen to that. Takes me back awhile, it does, miles back. Back to the days of mother and roses and ambitions and friends and spotless thoughts and collars. Maybe it's not such a terrible thing not to be able to get arrested. Maybe it's a sign—a directional gesticulation towards a new start. A New Road for Soapy Smith. A road paved with a real job and a roof over my head and great responsibilities—noble and ever-increasing responsibilities. Soapy Smith, man of position. Soapy Smith, a somebody in this world! (*Him appears behind Soapy as a policeman*)

HIM: Hey, bub. What are you doing here?

SOAPY (*brief pause, looks at the audience*): Then again, maybe not. (*Turns to him*) I'm doing nothing. You and me got that much in common.

HIM: Come along with me, jocko. You know what vagrancy and insulting an officer of the law can get you?

SOAPY (*hopefully*): Two months?

HIM: Maybe up to three.

SOAPY (*ecstatic; he pulls the policeman off*): And a Merry Christmas to you, too!!

HER (*to Jim*): I've heard there's a job opening at my husband's factory.

JIM: There is?

HER: I could ask him to put in a good word for you, if you'd like.

JIM: Della, do you hear that?

DELLA: That's wonderful!

JIM: What kind of position is it?

WILLY: Vice-president.

HER (*to Willy*): Don't get carried away. (*To Jim and Della*) It's the clerk in the purchasing department. Are you interested?

JIM: I sure am.

DELLA: Merry Christmas. (*Hugs Jim*)

JIM: Merry Christmas. (*They kiss*)

WILLY: Merry Christmas. (*Soapy bursts on stage; he is wearing a chain and ball*)

SOAPY: And a Happy New Year! (*Willy throws snow over Her*)

HER: SNOW!

ALL:

    YEARS FLY PAST AND SONGS ARE
       REARRANGED
    BUT THE SONGS THAT LAST LIKE THE FIRST
       GIFTS EXCHANGED
    COME FROM THE HEART, COME FROM THE
       HEART
    FROM THE HEART, FROM THE HEART

WILLY:

    THEY ARE GIVEN FROM THE HEART.

REPRISE: *GIFTS OF THE MAGI*

WILLY:

    AND THOUGH I SPEAK A PARABLE
    OF PEOPLE WHO WOULD FLY
    WOULD IT BE SO TERRIBLE TO TRY
    COME AND TRY, O
    WHAT COULD MAKE A KING
    TRAIL A STAR ABOVE?
    GIVE UP EVERYTHING
    MAYBE IT WAS LOVE
    LOVE IS WHAT WE BRING

ALL:

    AND THOUGH WE WILL NOT SWEAR A VOW
    THAT ALL WE TELL IS TRUE
    WE SWEAR IT ALL COULD HAPPEN NOW TO
       YOU
    ARE WE FACT, ARE WE MYTH
    WE WILL ANSWER YOU WITH
    JUST ONE

LOOK AND YOU WILL SEE
HOPE IS ALL AGLOW
DREAMS OF WHAT CAN BE
SETTLE LIKE THE SNOW
COULD YOU EVER GIVE
EVERYTHING YOU OWN.

EVERYTHING YOU TOUCH
ALL YOU'VE EVER LOVED
ALL YOU'VE EVER KNOWN
WOULD IT BE AS MUCH
AS THE GIFTS OF THE MAGI

(*Him and Her nod to Willy, smile and exit. Soapy tips his hat to Willy, exits. Jim and Della, his arm around her, exit through audience, smiling at Willy*)

WILLY:

WILL IT BE AS MUCH
AS THE GIFTS OF THE MAGI

(*After final note of the song, Willy gestures. Lights out.*)